The Silver Arrow

The Scout Association
25 Buckingham Palace Road,
London SW1W OPY.

The Silver Arrow

a voyage of discovery

Compiled by:
Michael Beach
Winnie Viner

Editors:
David Harwood
Valerie Peters

General Editor:
Ron Jeffries

Illustration:
Peter Harrison
Colin Watson

Design:
Colin Watson

SBN 85165 070 8

First Edition First Printing

January 1973

Printed in Great Britain by

**Page Bros (Norwich) Ltd.,
Norwich.**

Contents

The Silver Arrow

You have gained your Bronze Arrow and so now you are ready to set sail on the voyage of the Silver Arrow.

For the past few months you have been working hard at that Bronze Arrow, and what a lot of things you discovered—you had a lot of fun too. Everything you found out is going to be useful to you now, because the Silver Arrow is the next stage in your Cub Scout Programme. This time you will be discovering how to light a fire, cook sausages, visit a place of interest, make a wood model, entertain the Pack and many more exciting things. So here we go—off to discover the Silver Arrow. Are you ready?

The Map of your Voyage

1st Port

Health

(*a*) *Know why it is important to keep the feet in good condition.*
(*b*) *Know the importance of having a good night's sleep.*
(*c*) *Show what to do in the case of a nose-bleed.*
(*d*) *Know the importance of summoning adult help in cases of accident.*

Everybody wants to be healthy and by keeping some simple rules you can keep yourself fit.

Feet!

Have you ever thought about your feet? Have a look at them now, funny aren't they?, but very important too, just think how hard they work, so it's worth looking after them properly—they have to last a long time!

Here are some simple rules for keeping them in condition:

Wash them regularly, dry them thoroughly—especially between the toes.

Make sure that your shoes fit properly—not too tight, not too loose.

Change your socks regularly—especially if your feet get very hot.

Try some simple exercises to keep your feet in trim, like wriggling and stretching your toes, and picking up things with them.

You are going to need your feet for so many things so look after them **now.**

Sleep!

There are many times when we don't want to go to bed! But just think what we should be like if we never had enough sleep—bad tempered, not able to work properly, not wanting to eat much. Your body uses up lots of energy during the day and sleep is very important to give you the strength to do all the things you want to do.

Here are some simple rules to remember:

Have regular sleep—try and go to bed at the same time every night.

Have a warm milk drink before going to bed.

Use light, warm blankets.

Make sure some fresh air comes into the bedroom.

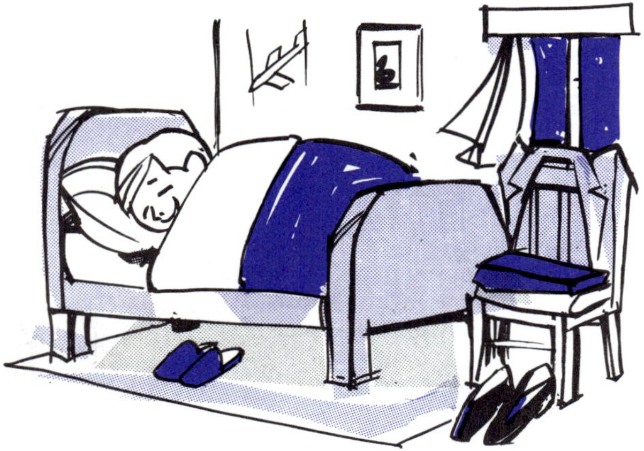

Nose Bleed!

Lots of people suffer from nose-bleeds, they look much worse than they are, and you can help to stop them. Don't panic, just follow the simple rules:

(1) Sit the patient down.
(2) Tip his head slightly forward.
(3) Tell him to breathe through his mouth.
(4) Grip or get him to grip, the fleshy part of the nose just below the bridge until the bleeding stops.
(5) Tell him not to blow his nose for a while afterwards.

The most important first-aid help you can give is to go and get adult help in an emergency. Either run to someone you know or tell someone near what the trouble is. Make sure that you know exactly where the accident is and that you give clear instructions to the people you are telling. By acting quickly you could help to save a life.

Badge Link

The badge that links with this is **First-Aider.** It is a very important badge. Perhaps you can begin to work on this now.

2nd Port

Feats of Skill

Either

(*a*) *Swim 10 metres*

Or

(*b*) 1. *Show that you have confidence in water by carrying out the following:*
Be able to walk backwards and forwards through the water.
Be able to put your face under water.
Be able to hold the bar and kick your feet up.
Be able to get into and out of the pool without using steps.
2. *Over a period of at least three months achieve, by means of regular practice, an improvement in your performance in three of the following activities:*
Skip 15 times forward and 15 times backwards, turning the rope yourself.
Balance along an edge such as a beam or brick wall not more than 13 cm (5 in) wide for at least 4.5 metres (15 ft).
Forward circle over a bar at least waist high.
Climb a ladder and a step ladder and know how to make sure that they are in a safe position.
Dribble a football out of doors, as quickly as you can around at least six obstacles over a distance of not more than 18 metres (20 yds).

Suppose you were lucky enough to be at camp on a hot summer's day and nearby was a sandy beach and cool blue sea—but you couldn't swim! Wouldn't that be awful? Or, perhaps you were walking by a river when you saw a young child fall in and you couldn't do anything, because you couldn't swim—wouldn't that be terrible? So you can see how important it is to learn to swim. It's fun and good exercise and it could save a life.

How will you learn to swim? Perhaps you are already swimming at school or perhaps Akela is taking you to a swimming pool. There is only one way to learn—and that is by getting into the water and practising!
Swimming Clubs are run in many places—and many pools have classes for non-swimmers. Have a look in the library or Town Hall and see if there are any lessons in your area.

Starting

You could begin to practise at home. Try breathing exercises—taking deep breaths and holding your breath. Try to practise the strokes by lying on a stool.
Get to a pool. Begin by just getting used to the water. Here are two exercises for you to practise:
1. Hold the rail, take a deep breath and put your face in the water for a short time. Lift your head so your mouth is free of the

water, breathe out, take another breath and put your face under again. Repeat the exercise.

2. Hold the rail, take a deep breath, put your face into the water, blow-out under the water. Lift your head so your mouth is clear of water, take another deep breath and do it again.

Learn to Float

Your body will float easily when you learn to relax enough. You could start by using air-rings, water wings etc. to get used to the water.

Learn to Tread Water

Use a breast-stroke leg kick and a 'sculling' motion with the hands to thrust the water downwards. Keep your nose and mouth clear of the water and your head tilted back. This will help you to get used to water and the swimming movements of the leg.

The Breast-Stroke: Follow the pictures and practise the movements until you get the idea.
If you were looking down on the top of a swimmer the stroke would look like this:—

Press with straight arms.

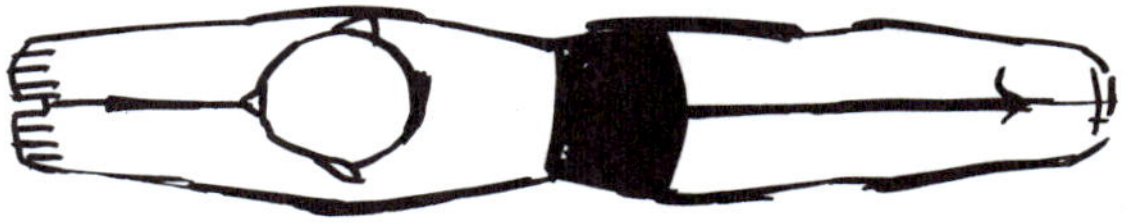

Elbows bent, bring thumbs together in front of your chin. Heels being drawn up towards your bottom.

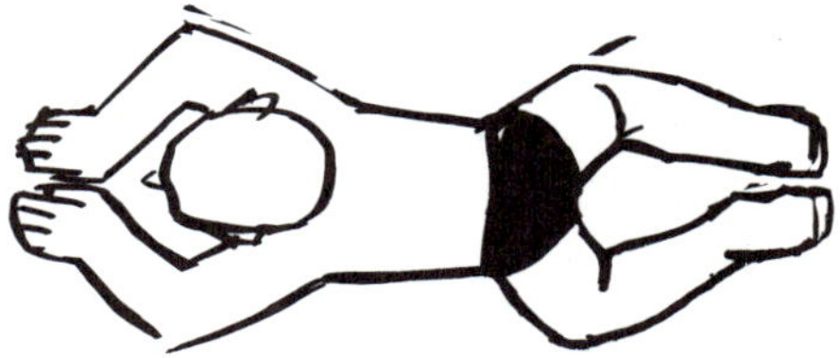

Arms pushing forwards just below the surface. Legs pushing backwards.

Complete the stroke.

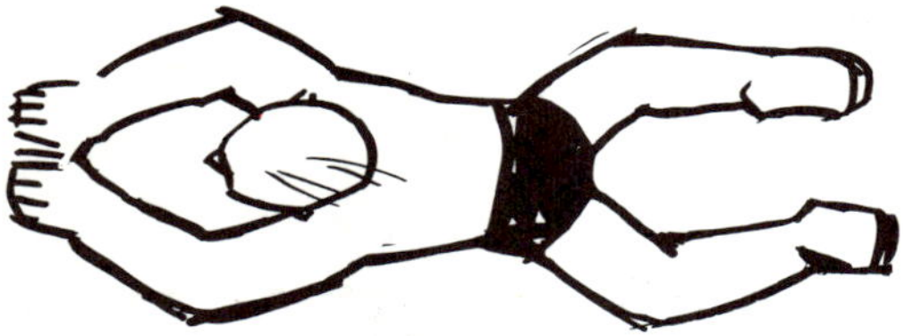

Badge. If you have any stage of the **Swimmers Badge** (and you can take this badge immediately after you are invested) then you will not have to pass this test, because you will have passed it already.

Non-Swimmers

Water Safety

This will help you to get used to water. It might also help you to start swimming. Start at the shallow end of the pool and never do the test in water that is more than waist high.

Everybody should try their hardest to pass the swimming part of the test because it is so very important. But if it is impossible for you to swim, perhaps because you cannot get to a pool, then you can do the other part of the test.

Skipping

Make sure the rope is not too long—knot the ends to give yourself something to hold. Don't forget the 'hop' between the skips! Boxers skip to keep fit, so at the third month you should be very fit!

Balance along an edge

Start by choosing a low wall. You can try higher walls as you get better. Or use a bench. Make sure that there is something soft to drop onto, either side. Time yourself and see if you get faster. Balance with your arms outstretched it if helps.

Forward Circle over a Bar

Make sure it's a neat clean roll each time. Again be sure that you land on soft ground.

Climb a ladder

It's important to know how to climb a ladder. Make sure all the rungs are tight and that the ladder is firm on the ground and doesn't wobble. Start by climbing a few steps at a time until you are used to it.

Dribble a Football

Here is something that's real fun. Practise hard and time yourself around the course. Don't hit the obstacles!

For all these tests you have to show that you are getting better at them over three months—so practise hard. Here's a chart to help you keep a record of how you get on. Mark in how good you are each month.

Month one	Month two	Month three

These are tests requiring lots of practise so start on them at the beginning of your Silver Arrow to give yourself plenty of time.
Try very hard to pass the swimming part—it will give you a lot of fun if you can swim.
Here's a certificate to fill in if you pass that part of Feats of Skill.

I swam 10 metres for my Silver Arrow on . . .

. . . .

at . . . .

Badge Link

All of these badges follow on from this test so perhaps you might try and take one of them. They are all useful to have.

Scout Link

For your Advanced Scout Standard in the Troop you will have to swim—so this test is good practice.

Athlete

Rescuer

Swimmer

Follow On

The 'Know the Game' book on Swimming will be very useful.

3rd Port

Exploring

Visit a place of local interest and report on what you have found out about it.

Do you know what an explorer is? He discovers a place nobody else has seen. Columbus discovered America, Captain Cook discovered Australia but what are you going to discover? It won't be easy to find some place in your town that hasn't yet been discovered, but perhaps you will be able to find out something about a place that wasn't known before.
What will you visit? Here are some ideas to help you wherever you live.

Local Church

How old is it?
Who is it named after?
Who is the Vicar?
What is special about it?
Are there any interesting monuments?

New Area

How many houses are there?
How many flats?
What are the roads named after?
Who built the flats?
Is there anything special near them—such as a playground or park?
Are there any shops nearby?

Old House

When was it built?
Who built it?
Who has lived there?
Has anybody famous stayed there?
How big is it?
Is there anything special in the house?
What should you especially look for?

Old Site

Perhaps a stone circle or a burial barrow.
The site of an old windmill, a house or a Roman camp.

It doesn't have to be an old place, just an interesting one. Here are some more places you could find out about.

A Library
A School
A Park
A Local Factory
A Local Shop
Where can you find out about the place you choose?
Find a local map and see what you can discover.
Talk to your Minister, Vicar or the Church Verger.
Talk to some older people who have lived in the town for some time.
Get a town guide (available from local newsagents or the library).
How will you present to Akela the things you have found out?

Here are some ideas:

A Log-book: An old exercise book in which you paste pictures of the place, and write down things you have found out about it. You could put in any interesting information you have discovered.

A Tape-recording: If you have the use of a tape-recorder you could tape the story of your discovery and play it back to the Pack or Akela.

Take Pictures: If you can borrow a camera you could take photographs of the place and anything around it. It could make an interesting collection and you can show them to Akela as you tell him what you have found out.

Tell Akela: Just tell Akela everything you have found out. Collect any postcards, brass rubbings, leaflets or anything else to make it more interesting.

Check Card.

Here's a check card to help you when you have chosen the place you are going to explore.

The Place: . . . .

Where it is: . . . .

How old: . . . .

Who built it: . . . .

Some interesting things about it: . . . .

. . . .

Some people who lived there: . . . .

. . . .

Some pictures . . . .

Scout Link

In your Scout Standard you will be finding out about local areas so this test will help you in the Troop.

Follow On

Some books which might be helpful to you:

Arthur Mee County Books
Town Guide
I Spy Books
Pitman books of Cathedrals and Towns.

4th Port

Discovering Nature

(*a*) *Grow something such as cress or other quick growing seed.*
(*b*) *Know the type of food to give to birds in winter.*

What do you think of when someone says 'Nature'? Do you think of something that can only be seen in the country? Well, nature is everywhere and this part of the voyage is going to help us to find out something about it.

Have you ever grown anything? A plant, a bulb or perhaps flowers from seed, well, if you have, you will remember how from something quite small there grows something very large, in quite a short time. But it doesn't just happen, all plants need warmth, light and water to make them grow.

You are going to grow something for this test so you will see it all happening.

Here are some things that you could grow

Cress You can buy a packet of cress for about 4p. All it needs to grow is a piece of damp flannel and plenty of light.

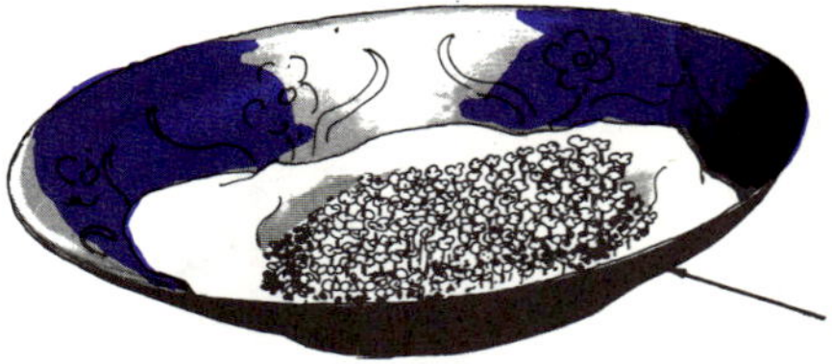

Keep it in the light and watch it grow.

Monster

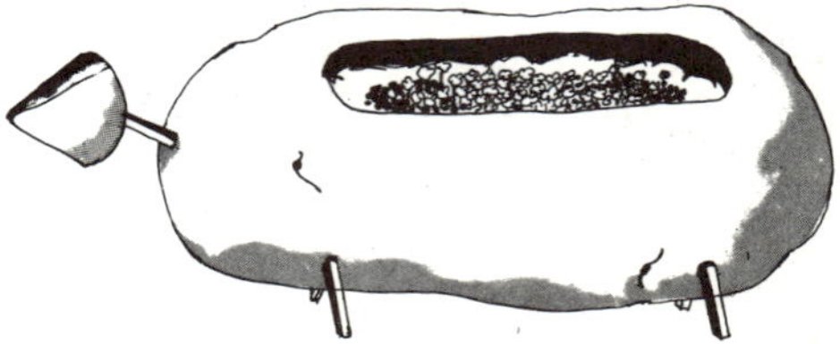

When the cress grows the 'monster' will have a green furry back!

Your Name

Borrow a tray or large plate. Put flannel on it and make sure it is kept damp. Sprinkle cress in the shape of your name and watch your name grow in cress.

Bean

A bean will grow quickly—you can almost see it grow.

Here's what to do:

1. Take a jam jar.
2. Put a piece of rolled blotting paper inside the jar—*keep it damp*.
3. Put a bean between the jar side and the blotting paper.
4. Keep it in the light and watch it grow.

After a while you will see the bean sprout. See how tall it will grow. You could, when it is big enough, transplant it into the garden.

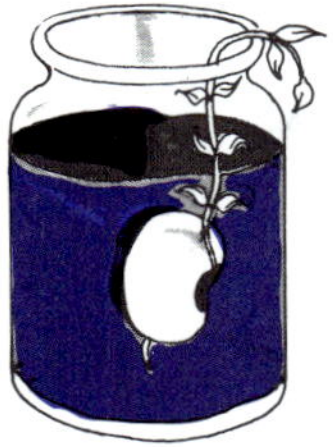

Carrot Top

Slice the top off a carrot, stand it in a saucer of water and watch it grow. After a day or two it will sprout.
See what other tops will sprout, perhaps turnips, swedes, onions, beetroots.

Potato

Take a potato that is sprouting and a shoe box.

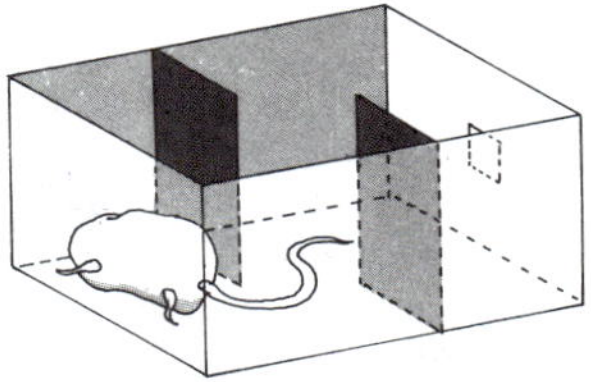

Prepare the box as shown above and place the potato inside.
Put the lid on the box, stand the hole towards the light, take the lid off from time to time. You will see the potato sprout twisting around the walls to get to the light.

What do birds eat in winter time?

In the Spring, Summer and Autumn there is plenty for birds to eat; insects; berries; fruit and seeds, but in the Winter, especially if its very cold, there's not so much food to be found. That is the time you can help by making sure they do get something to eat.

Here are some things they will eat.
Bacon Fat: For Blue-Tits, Coal-Tits, Greenfinches. Leave it uncut and tie it to the fence or tree bough with string. They will like to swing on the rind as they eat it.
For other birds chop up the fat into small bits and put it on your birdtable.
Pastry and Bread: Scraps of raw pastry are very popular so is bread. But cut it up well before you put it out.
Nuts, Currants, Raisins: Birds will like to eat nuts—string them up for the Blue-Tits etc. and leave them loose for the others. Currants and raisins are also good for them.
Scraps: The odd bits left after meals, cooked potato, vegetables etc, well chopped up, will disappear quickly.
Coconut: If you can get a coconut (perhaps you might win one) put half of it out for the birds. They will enjoy nibbling away at the nut.
Water: Don't forget that birds also need drink. A small dish of water should be left for them—make sure it doesn't ice over.

Bird Table

Perhaps you could make a bird table to put the food on. A square plywood top, about 45 × 60 cm (18 in × 24 in) screwed onto a broom handle, or a straight piece of 5 × 5 cm (2 in × 2 in) wood,

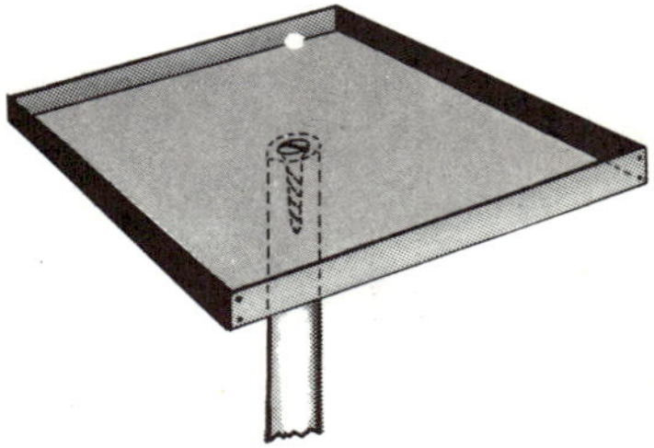

then dug into the ground is a simple way to do it. Put an edge around the table so that the food doesn't blow away.

Perch

A perch—a piece of dowel rod drilled into the fence—makes a simple bird food store, hang bacon fat and nuts from it.

Look for the birds who come and feed. The birds that stay with us in the winter are Sparrows, Blue-Tits, Coal-Tits, Wrens, Greenfinches, Robins, Starlings and Thrushes. See how many you can spot.

Badge Link

Naturalist Badge will help you to discover a lot about nature.

Follow On

Some useful books are: Ladybird Nature Books
Observer Nature Books

Visit a nature or bird reserve.

5th Port

Safety

Know the Water Safety Rules

Well, you have done the swimming test and this test tells you how to make sure you will always be safe in water and also help others to know how to behave in water.
It is a lot of fun playing about, swimming around and enjoying being in water—especially on a hot day! But it can be dangerous. The water safety rules are just commonsense to make certain that you are never a nuisance or a danger when you are in the water. What are the water safety rules? Here they are:

If you fall into the water and cannot swim

Keep calm, call for help.

Try and float, don't throw your arms about.

If someone else falls in

Find a stout stick, scarf or something to help pull him to the bank.

Fetch help at once if you are with someone else or send them for help.

Tell the person in the water to float, if he can.

Floats can be dangerous

Be careful with floats, never go out of your depth.

Rivers and Gravel Pits can be dangerous

Gravel pits have steep banks and can be very deep. Rivers also can have steep banks. Never play in gravel pits and be very careful near rivers.

Keep within your depth

Bathe Safely

Ask your parents if it is safe for you to go in. Never bathe immediately after a meal. Always swim with others. Come out before you get tired.
Here are a couple of ideas to help you remember the rules and to show Akela that you know them.

Water Safety Television

1. Get an empty shoe box and cut out a 'screen'.
2. Take two lengths of dowel rod and make four holes—at the top and bottom of the box, two on either side. Poke the rods through these.

3. Get a long roll of paper, or stick several sheets together with sticky tape. They must all be narrower than the width of the box.
4. Draw pictures on the paper to show various rules of the safety code. Each picture should be big enough to fill the 'screen'.

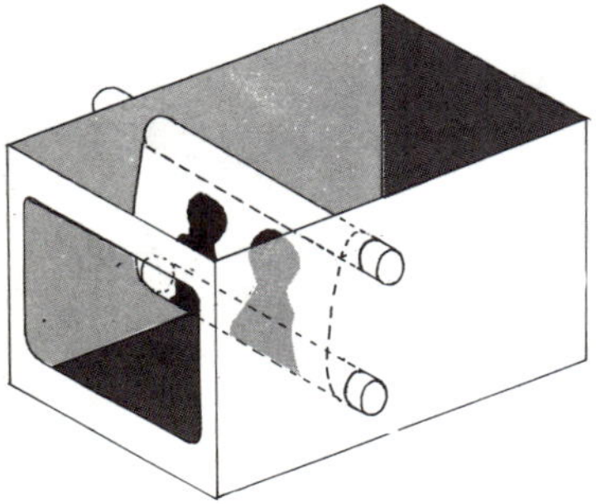

5. Stick one end of the paper to the bottom rod and roll it on until the last picture is reached, then stretch the paper up and stick the end to the top rod. Rather like putting a film into a camera.

By turning the rods you can move the pictures onto the screen. Make all the pictures as large and colourful as possible.

Shadowgraph

A Shadowgraph is made by making a screen from a white sheet or a piece of white paper, with a strong light shining from behind.

By cutting out card figures and putting them onto sticks you have puppets and can show them as large shadows by inserting them between the light and the screen. Make a 'shadow play' about the safety rules—practise with coloured paper to get the effect of water.

6th Port

Service

(*a*) *Be able to use a public telephone, a directory and code book correctly.*
(*b*) *Know how to make an emergency call and find the nearest telephone.*
(*c*) *Carry a message containing dates, figures and names.*

As part of your Promise you promise that you will help other people, but it is not much use saying you will help others unless you know how to do it. This test helps you to be of service so that you know what to do when someone asks for your help.

Public Telephone

You know what a telephone box is! There are many of them around the streets of every town, but do you know how to use them? This is what they look like inside:

How do you make a call?

1. Make sure that you know the number you want.
2. Pick up the telephone.
3. Dial the number.
4. It will ring, and when the person answers you will hear a funny bleeping noise—a series of rapid pips—put the 2p piece in immediately. You cannot be heard until the money has been put in.
5. If it is engaged you will get an engaged buzz, a single repeated note. Try again later.
6. If the number is not on STD then dial 100 and ask the Operator for the number you want. He will tell you how much money to put in.

Some General tips

Always speak slowly and clearly.
When answering the 'phone give your number and name.
Don't spend too long in a public call box—others might want to use it.

Practice—Ring Akela from a telephone box.
or —Find two boxes near to each other. Take the telephone numbers and get a friend to wait in one and ring him. Then let him ring you. **Never do this if people are waiting to use the box—remember as a Cub Scout you help others.**

Most telephone exchanges in the country are all-number exchanges. The Code Book gives you the name of every exchange with the code beside it so that you can find the number you want. The number is the exchange number and NOT the person's telephone number. For large towns there is a number at the beginning to give you the town. This is when a town has more than one exchange.

London	**Exchange No.**	**Telephone Number**
01	**111**	**3212**
Manchester	**Exchange No.**	**Telephone Number**
061	**212**	**3313**

All the information on exchange numbers is in the book. All the towns are in alphabetical order and there is a code book for every town. At the front of it you will find local exchanges for which you don't need a town number only the exchange.
For instance, if you lived in Glasgow and wanted to dial someone in Shettleston (a district of Glasgow), you would dial 778 followed by the number. If you lived in London and wanted to do that, you would dial 041 – 778 followed by the number.
To find out someone's telephone number you need a telephone directory. This is the big book found in call boxes and post offices. Most boxes will only have the local telephone directory. All the names are in alphabetical order, so you need to know the name and initial of the person and their address.
Practice looking for someone, perhaps Akela or Skip in your local directory so you get used to using it.

Services There are lots of services you can get by dialling certain numbers. If you don't know the telephone number of the person you require you can ring Directory Enquiries. You can also find out the test score, the weather, hear a pop-song and other information too. Look up the services in your Code Book.

Emergency Calls

If you need to ring the Police, Ambulance or Fire Station in an emergency you use the Emergency Service.
Pick up the phone.
Dial 999.
When the Operator answers tell him the service you require.

When that service answers tell them:—

What the emergency is.
Where it is.
How to get to it.
Who you are and where you are telephoning from (in case they want to ask you any more questions).

Important:

In an emergency call make sure you speak slowly and clearly.

How would you find the nearest telephone?

You might know that there is a call box near you, but supposing you don't know, how would you find the nearest 'phone?

At one time you could see the wires going to a house—but many lines are underground now. Just think of places that might have a 'phone—a café, a shop, bus or railway station, police station, cinema, post office, so even in an emergency you should be able to find a telephone. In an emergency you can knock at a house and ask politely if they have a 'phone—then explain why you want to know.

Carry a Message in your Head.

How many times have you forgotten a message Akela has given you—or Mum has asked you to remember? Never—well you will easily pass this test! But if you have, this test will help.

Start by remembering simple messages like:— 'At 3.0 o'clock on Saturday 15th May we are meeting at the hall for a party'. You won't forget that! Get someone to make up harder messages for you to remember, or write a message down in the morning and see if you can remember it when you come home from school. The messages can get harder until you think you are good enough to pass the test.

Message (write it here)

all of it	**Remembered half of it**	**quarter of it**

Two ticks out of three in column one makes you quite good.

A Game

Try this game with some of your friends:

Form a circle. One person has a message he whispers to the boy next to him who whispers it to the next until it goes right round the circle and back to the beginning

You will be surprised at how the message ends up!

Scout Link

This test will be helpful to you in the Troop when you are doing your **Scout Standard.**

Follow On

Why not get Akela to take you to a telephone exchange to see how it works?

7th Port

Flags and Countries

(*a*) *Tell the stories of the Patron Saints of England, Ireland, Scotland and Wales and know their special days, emblems and flags.*
(*b*) *Know the composition of the Union Flag.*

A Patron Saint is the Saint that is looked upon as the extra-special protector of a country. In the United Kingdom we have four Patron Saints, one for each country.
Here are the stories of the Saints. Perhaps you could act the stories with your Six or with other Cub Scouts in the Pack. You could make simple props like armour, swords, crowns etc. to make it even more interesting and show Akela how much you know.

St. George of England.

St. George grew up in Rome and became a well known soldier of the Emperor. There was a law at that time which said that all Christians must be killed. George begged the Emperor to spare their lives and in the end gave up being a soldier to spend all his time helping the Christians, which was a very dangerous thing to do. The Emperor was so angry that he ordered George to be beheaded.
A legend about George tells how he was journeying to see the Emperor Diocletian and pleaded with him for the lives of the Christians. When one day, he came upon a town which was being terrorised by a ferocious dragon all the people in the town kept feeding it on sheep, until all the sheep had gone and they had to choose someone among them to sacrifice.

The King's daughter was chosen and taken to the dragon's cave to await her death. Then George came riding by and asked her why she was so frightened, so she told him about the dragon. 'I will kill the dragon in the name of Jesus' said George. Then the dragon came out of the cave, looking very fierce and George took his lance and killed him, thus saving the Princess.
The King was so overjoyed at what George had done in the name of Jesus, that he and many of his people became Christians and he built a Church in George's memory.
Many years later the Crusaders, were fighting the heathen Saracens in the Holy Land and they were inspired by the story of St. George which they brought back with them to England, where George became the Patron Saint.
The flag of St. George came from this time too, as the Crusaders wore white surcoats over their armour, which were emblazoned with a large red cross, and these came to be associated with the Saint.

St. Patrick of Ireland

Patrick is said to have been born in Scotland and captured by pirates and taken to Ireland. He was sold as a slave and spent six years looking after pigs. During this time he never lost the Christian faith which he had as a boy.
Eventually he escaped to France where he trained as a priest. After many years he was ordained as a Bishop and decided to return to Ireland. He arrived at Eastertime and the Irish people were celebrating one of their heathen festivals. The Druids, who were their priests, had forbidden any fires to be lit, but Patrick ignored this, he lit a fire which drew all the people to him out of curiosity.

Then he preached to them about the Christian faith and showed them how God is 'three in one' by picking a native plant, the Shamrock, which had three parts to the one leaf. Patrick converted many of them including their chieftain.
He travelled around the land telling the people about God, building churches and being a friend to everyone whom he met.
Legend says that Patrick drove all the snakes from Ireland with his Bishop's staff. We don't know if that is true, but it's a nice legend.

St. Andrew of Scotland

Andrew was one of the first disciples to follow Jesus. He was a fisherman on the Sea of Galilee with his brother Simon Peter. After Andrew had seen Jesus, he told his brother all about him.
One day, Jesus passed by the brothers working on their boat and said to them — 'Follow me and I will make you fishers of men'.
The two brothers followed Jesus and spent the rest of their time with him.
After Jesus was crucified, Andrew travelled around the country telling people about him.
The favourite story about St. Andrew is when the disciple received a call for help from his friend Matthew who was sick in prison in a distant land.
Andrew wanted to go to his rescue but he had no boat, then by chance he came upon a boat and a stranger who offered to sail it for him. That night a great storm came up, but Andrew fell asleep. When he awoke he found that the boat had crossed the seas safely, but the stranger had disappeared, then he realised that the

stranger had been Jesus. At length Andrew arrived at his journey's end and was able to persuade the people to release Matthew. Matthew insisted on staying to work among the people and Andrew had to travel back to Achaia; there he found all his work destroyed and he was persecuted and crucified.

The cross Andrew was crucified on was diagonal—in the shape of and X and this is why St. Andrew's flag is like that. Nine hundred years later St. Andrew's bones were brought from Greece and buried in that place in Scotland now called St. Andrews.

St. David of Wales

Even when David was a boy, he loved God. He was a happy-go-lucky boy with a good singing voice, like so many Welsh people. David grew up in the service of God and was educated by monks. One of the monks taught David all about the bible and legend says that this monk was going blind, but David touched his eyes and brought back his sight. When David grew up he became a monk himself and travelled about Wales telling people about God.

One of the monasteries where he lived is now called St. Davids and has a fine cathedral. His fame gradually spread and when, at a great gathering, one of the Bishops could not be heard, he sent for David who immediately quietened the people and told them all about God's love. It was said that after he spoke a white dove alighted on his shoulder. David later became Archbishop for South Wales and when he died, an old man, he had founded many monasteries and given his country peace in troubled times.

Each Saint has a special flag and emblem, as well as their own day.

St. George — England — Saints Day 23rd April

The cross of St. George the English flag.

Rose — the emblem of England

Here is a dragon to remind you of the legend of St. George.

St. Patrick — Ireland — Saints Day 17th March

The flag of St. Patrick for Northern Ireland.

Shamrock — the emblem of Ireland.

Legend says that Patrick used this to explain the Trinity — Father, Son and Holy Ghost.

Here is a Bishop's hat called 'a Mitre'. St. Patrick was the first Bishop of Ireland.

St. Andrew — Scotland — Saints Day 30th November

The cross on which St. Andrew was crucified — the flag of Scotland.

Thistle — the emblem of Scotland.

Legend says that once when the Scots were at war, their enemies tried to creep up on them one night. In order not to make any noise they took their shoes off. However one unfortunate man trod on a thistle and let out a cry of pain which awoke the sleeping Scots, who then fought off their enemies.

Here is the fish which is used to represent St. Andrew, this was also a symbol of the early Christians.

St. David — Wales — Saints Day 1st March

The Welsh flag is not a cross and therefore cannot be used in the Union Flag, but it is a splendid red dragon on a white and green background.

Leek — the emblem of Wales.

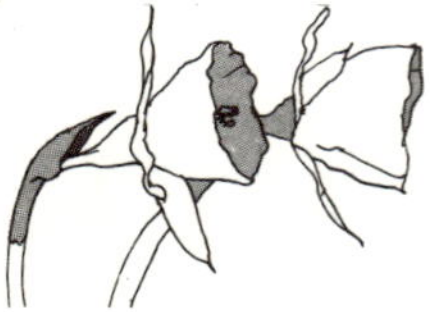

Legend says that St. David tended the gardens of the Monastery, and grew wild leeks as vegetables.
Daffodil — this is sometimes used as symbol of Wales and it reminds us of the pleasant Welsh green mountains and valleys.

You could display the three flags on card to pass your test, showing the emblem, the flag and a drawing of the Saint.

or

You could make a plasticine model of a scene from a Saint's life, showing the flag and emblem.

or

You can make flag cards.
Take a postcard and colour it blue. Cut it diagonally in four so that you have four triangles as shown in the diagram. Fold over the longest side of each triangle, then taking another postcard stick the flap of each triangle to one edge of the card, so that it will represent the flag of St. Andrew. This can of course be done for the other flags. Under each blue triangle draw, on the bottom card, something which will remind you of the Saint.

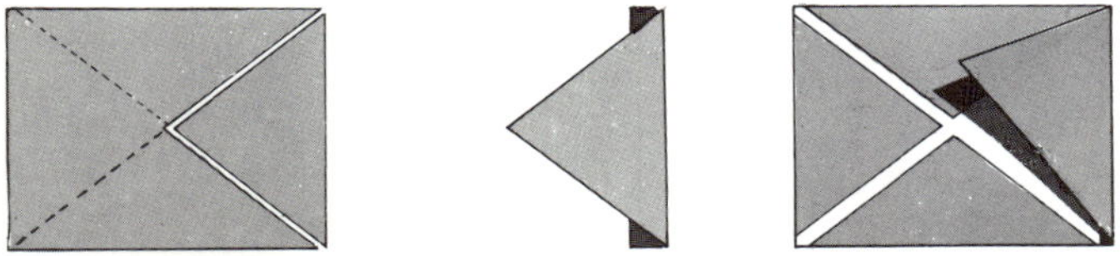

The Union Flag

The Union Flag—or Union Jack as it is usually called—is the National flag of Great Britain. It is flown at Pack Meeting, Scout camps and you see it flying from buildings on special days, like the Queen's birthday.
It is one flag made up from the three flags of England, Scotland and Northern Ireland.
When the flag is flying from a pole or mast it is flown with the broad white band at the top .If it is flown the other way round it is a sign of distress.
The Union Flag grew from one flag to three like this:—

In 1606 the first Union Flag was made by putting the English and Scottish Flags together like this

Then in 1801 the Flag of Northern Ireland was added to make the Union Flag we have today.

Why not make up your own special prayer for each of the Saints. You could say it at the end of a Pack Meeting and you could make one up asking God's blessings on Great Britain and for peace in the world.

My Prayer about St. George

My Prayer about St. Andrew

My Prayer about St. David

My Prayer for the Country and for Peace.

My Prayer about St. Patrick

Follow-On

Two books you will find useful:
Ladybird book of Saints
Ladybird book of Flags

8th Port

Handcraft

either

(*a*) *Make a model, using balsa wood, polystyrene or other materials:*

or

(*b*) *Assemble a construction kit and finish it to a good standard.*

Do you know what balsa wood is? It's a very light wood, a big block weighs practically nothing, so it is particularly useful for model making -- you can use it for making gliders or model planes. Where do you get it? Well any model-shop will have a selection of balsa wood in all sizes and lengths.
First of all, you will need to decide just what you are going to make. As it's a very soft wood, a sharp modelling knife and some sandpaper are about the only tools you will need.
Here are some ideas for you to try!

A Statue

Balsa wood is so soft that if you got a block of it you could make a head, or an animal statue by deciding on the shape it is to take, cutting away until you have the rough outline and then sandpapering it to the final shape.
Stick the statue onto a base—it could make a nice present.

Glider

Take a thick piece of balsa wood, shape it into a plane body with sandpaper—you could cut away the edges to save some time. Stick on two wings (use thin balsa wood). Stick on the tail. You will need a weight on the nose, paper clips are ideal. Practise to see how it glides. It must be balanced, so you might need to adjust the weight.

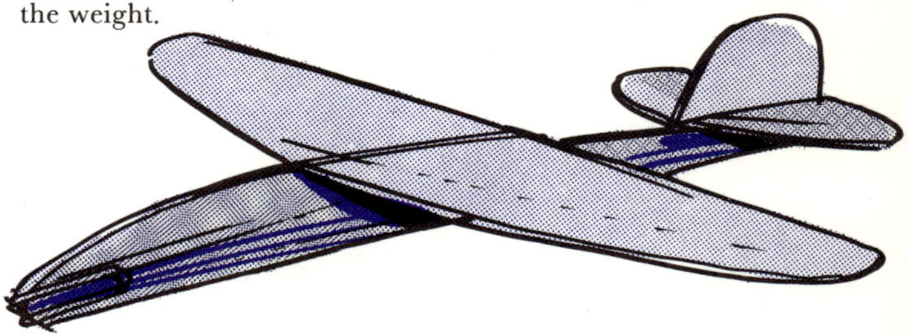

A Kite

The frame of a kite can be made from balsa wood sticks, as it is so light.

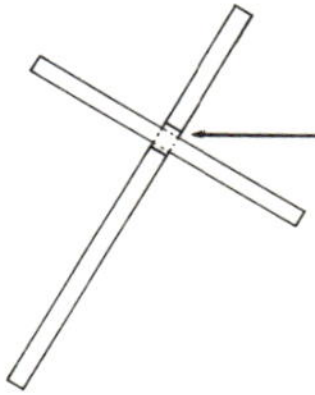

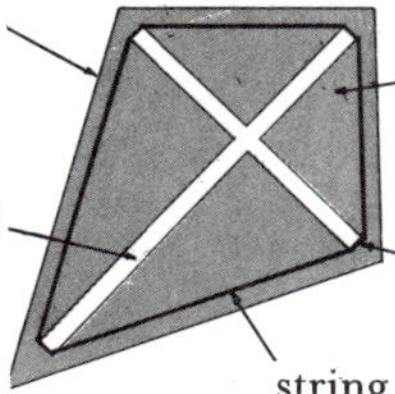

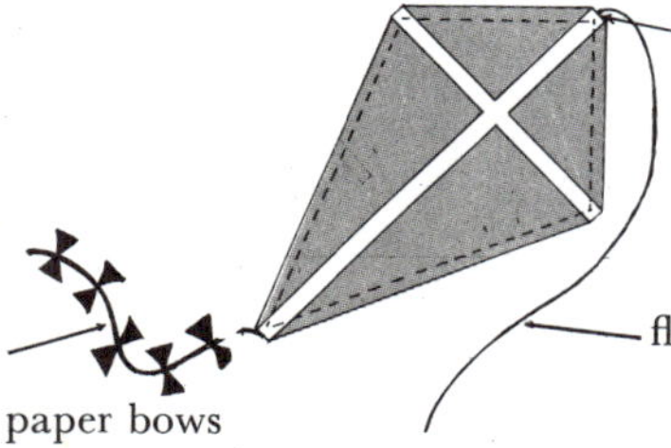

Take the kite to a hill when there is some wind—see how well it flies!

Polystyrene

Polystyrene is also very light. It is best known by the tiles you stick onto the ceiling, but you can get it in blocks.
To stick it you will need special polystyrene glue, since ordinary glue melts the polystyrene!
You can also get cutters which work from a battery and this means that you can cut very fine shapes from the polystyrene. They look like this.

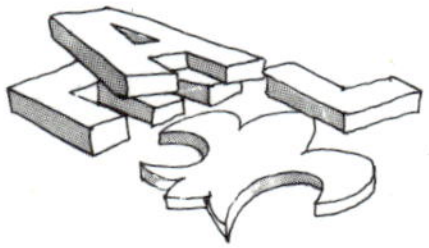

Here's some things you can make.

Modern Art

If you can get some really thick blocks of polystyrene you could make a modern art decoration.

You will need a hot spike (a soldering iron is ideal, ask Dad to show you how to use it).

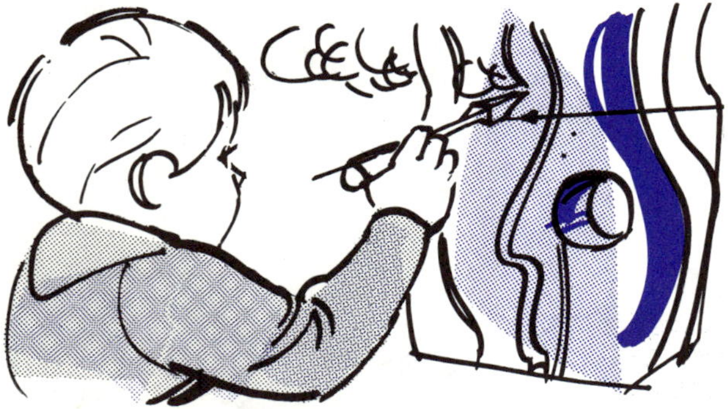

Block of polystyrene, about 1 metre (3 ft.) high. Run the soldering iron down the sides to make a decorative pattern (the material will melt as you touch it).

You could make cut out shapes.

Paint the block with bright water-colours. You will have an attractive modern art decoration for a present.

Make a 'Polystyrene Rubbing'

You have seen the wall pictures of saints or soldiers from brass rubbings, well here is another kind of picture.

You will need:

A sheet of black paper.

Thin polystyrene roll, as used for walls.

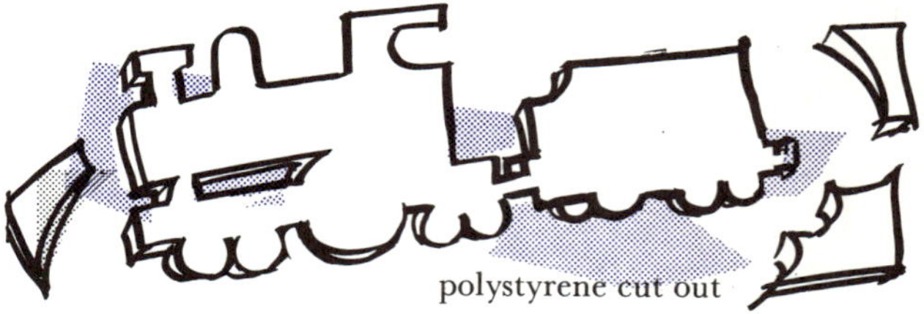

Cut out the shape you want, an engine or perhaps one of the Patron Saints—stick onto it the black paper and you have an unusual decoration.

Place Mats

Take some polystyrene ceiling tiles. With your cutter you can cut out shapes—colour them with paint and you have an attractive place mat. Here are some ideas for shapes:

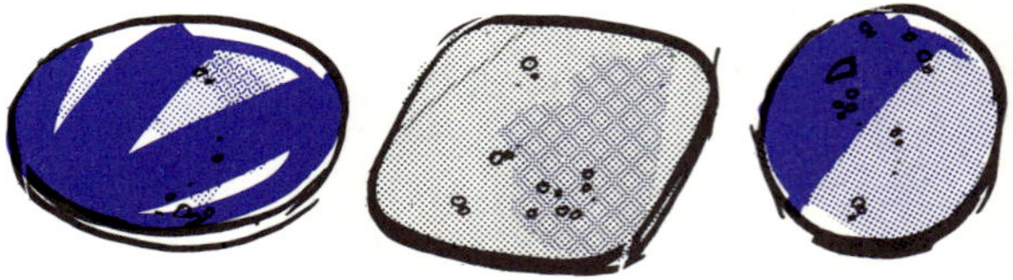

A Model from a Kit

There are hundreds of kits these days to make all kinds of things from model cars, aeroplanes or boats to pre-historic animals!

If you decide to do this test then the model you make will have to be the most difficult you can do and be done to the very best of your ability.

Perhaps you are already making models of a particular kind so you will probably make another to add to the collection. You could perhaps make a display of all the ones you have made.

Remember to:

Follow the instructions properly and make sure you complete all the detail.

Finish it off to the highest standard you can.

Make something that interests you.

Use the correct glue and the proper paints to finish it with.

9th Port

Out of Doors

Light a fire and cook sausages on it.
Know how to put out the fire and leave the site clean and tidy.

Here's an exciting test! Cooking sausages out in the woods on a fire you have lit yourself. You could get some of the Scouts to help you with this test. They should know all about fire-lighting.

But you must make sure that you start the fire properly because fire can be very dangerous and get out of control if you are not careful. Here are some simple rules for fire-lighting:—

1. Make sure that you are allowed to light fires in the place you are in.
2. Find a clearing away from trees or bushes in case these catch fire.
3. Dig out a square for the fire, either by lifting the turf or by clearing leaves and earth to make a pit.

4. Collect your wood and have a wood pile—otherwise your fire might go out while you are searching for more wood. You will need:

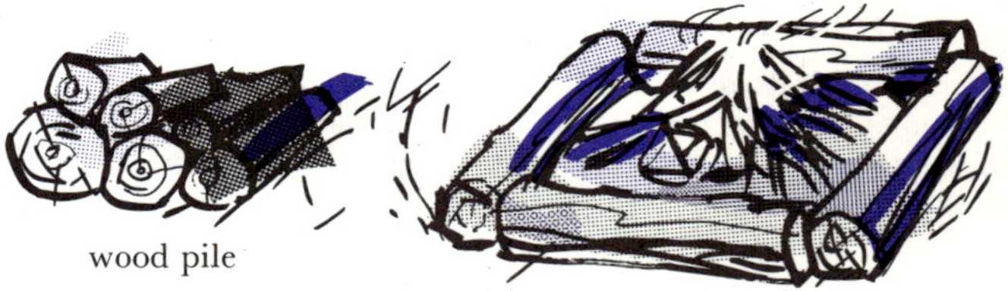

5. Put the large logs at the side of the pit, to keep the fire in
6. Make balls of paper and put them in the trench with the small twigs around them.
   Then light the fire (make sure the box of matches is kept away).
7. Slowly feed the fire with bigger and bigger pieces of wood until the fire is really going well.
8. To cook sausages you need a fire of glowing embers so put on one or two logs until it is going well and you have plenty of nice hot red ash.

Remember:
Use dry wood.
Don't use 'green' wood.
Don't pull branches from trees—it hurts the tree and won't burn properly anyway!

Cooking the sausages

Get a thick 'green stick' from the base of a tree, or neatly cut a small branch about 50 cm (18 in) long from a bush or tree. Peel off the bark to halfway up and sharpen one end. Put the sausage on and hold it over the red embers—an old fork is even better, so long as you wear a glove to hold it when the metal gets hot.

After you have finished

Make sure the fire is right out, you can pour water on it, if you have some **or**
Cover it with earth.
Put the larger unburnt or slightly burnt wood back into the undergrowth if it is not still warm. If there is any risk of it being hot, just stack it neatly and leave it.
Clear the pit.
Carefully put back the turf and tread it back.
The test is to make it seem as if there has been no fire there.
If you can get it like that then you have done a good job.

Something for you to try at home.

To practise outdoor cooking without a fire make a 'candle fire'. It's fun and will get you used to outdoor cooking!
Here's how you make it!

1. An old cocoa or coffee tin.
2. Punch fairly large holes all round the side about 2.5 cm (1 in) or so from the top.
3. Put a lighted candle under the tin (the holes make sure that air will keep it alight).

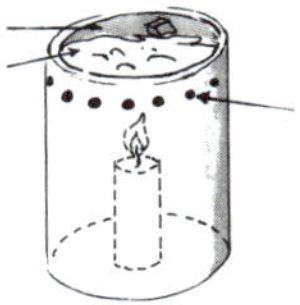

4. Make a pancake batter of flour and water.
5. Put a little fat on the tin top.
6. Pour on the batter, cook, turn and cook both sides.
7. Eat.

Badge Link

Explorer

This badge is very exciting—making shelters, lighting fires, following tracks.

Scout Link

Get a Scout to help you with the test. You will need to know how to light fires in the Troop, when you are at camp and on hikes.

10th Port

Entertaining

Do one of the following alone or with another Cub Scout.
(*a*) *Perform a Trick (scientific or conjuring).*
(*b*) *Tell a story or recite a poem.*
(*c*) *Sing a song.*
(*d*) *Play an instrument.*
(*e*) *Perform a series of tumbling tricks.*

First of all decide if you are going to do this test on your own or with someone else because you will need to practise to get it quite right.

Here are some things you could do:

Conjuring Tricks
Take the Ring off the String

Make a loop of string 2/3 metres (2 ft) long. Put a curtain ring on the loop. Ask someone to hold the loop as shown.

Halfway between the ring and one finger pick up the string and bring it round to loop over the opposite finger underneath.

Then, slip off. The ring will come off but the loop will stay.

Mind Reading

This needs two people. Get two telephone directories exactly the same. One person 'hides' behind something so he can't be seen. The conjurer in front tells the audience he can mind-read and to prove it he will tell them the actual name, address and telephone number of someone—anyone they choose. Then he asks the audience to pick a name from the book by calling out the page number, column, and number of lines from top. The person 'hiding' looks up the reference and whispers it so that only the conjurer can hear. He then announces the name and address to the audience.

The audience should be amazed! See how long it is before they discover how it is done.

Scientific Marvel

A candle burning under water! Impossible you say? Well it can be done.

1. Fill a bucket with water.
2. Float on the top a large cork or a small piece of wood.
3. Put a candle stump on it (hold it upright by melting some wax).
4. Light the candle and place a large jam jar over it.
5. Push the jar sharply down and you will see the candle burning under the water! It will only last for a while until the oxygen is all burnt, but at least you have proved that it can be done.

Your eyes deceive you.

Your eyes sometimes make things seem different than they are. Try these on the Pack:

The hat is taller than it is wide. Is it?

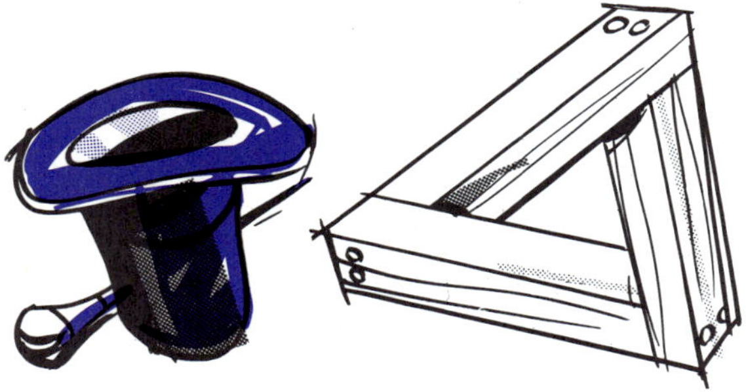

All of these are the same size. Measure them.
Cut out three strips of black paper exactly the same length but make one half the width of the other two. Decieve the eyes of the Pack with various arrangements of the strips.

Tell a Story or Recite a Poem

Choose the story or poem carefully.
Make sure it's one you like.
Practise it at home. Get all the various voices and tone of voice quite right, so that those listening know the different people in the story.
Try reading it in front of a mirror so that it looks right. See if you can get the right expressions for the various things happening. If possible, see if you can read it to a tape-recorder so you can hear yourself.

Tumbling Tricks

This can be fun. Do this—if you choose it—with another Cub. Practise the tricks with him. Build up a small display of different tricks, cartwheels, jumping over one and doing a head-over-heels. Make sure you have mats to do the tricks on.

Sing a Song or Play an Instrument

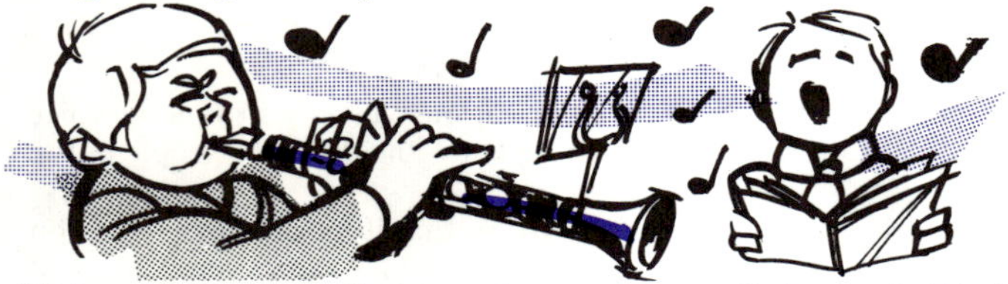

Make certain you really know the tune—and all the words if it is a song. Try and choose a tune or song that the Pack knows so that it can join in.
See if you can get one of the Venture Scouts to play a guitar accompaniment for you.
Don't make it too long.
Practise hard at home before you perform.

Presentation

See if you can do this test at the same time as others are doing it. Ask Akela to make it into a Pack Concert.
Have the Pack sitting down to watch. Have a programme. You could write one out on a poster so that everybody knows what is coming.
Have an announcer to announce the turns. It could be Akela. See if you can have it at one end of the hall with the lights on so that it becomes a stage. Perhaps you are lucky enough to have a stage to perform on.
Or you could present your item at the sing-song or camp fire. Perhaps the Concert could be on Parents' Evening?

Programme Poster

Silver Arrow Concert

1. Announcer — Jimmy
2. A Song — Trevor
3. Some Tricks — John
4. A Tune — Phillip

The End

Badge Link

Entertainer—is the badge that links with this. Have a look and see if you might become an Entertainer.

Scout Link

There will be lots of camp fires in the Troop. Now you can help to entertain at them. Perhaps the Scouts could help you to present a song for the Pack.

11th Port

Knotting

(*a*) *Tie a round turn and two half-hitches and a sheet-bend and demonstrate their use.*
(*b*) *Make sure you can still do your Bronze Arrow knots.*

Why bother with knots? Well think how often you are likely to need them. In the Scouts or at camp, and on many other occasions especially if you like fishing or sailing.

The time may come when you need a knot to help save a life or for use in first aid.

So knotting is very important.

What is a knot—it is a way of tying two ends of a rope to make sure that they stay joined and do not slip.

A Knot is a means of tying a loop.

A Bend fastens two ropes together.

A Hitch secures a rope to another object.

You need to know how to tie a sheet bend and a round turn and two half-hitches.

Make sure the ropes you are using are proper ropes and not odd pieces of string.

Make sure they are long enough for proper use.

It's a good idea to use different coloured ropes as it is easier to see how the knot is made.

Sheet Bend—for tying two ropes of different thickness together.

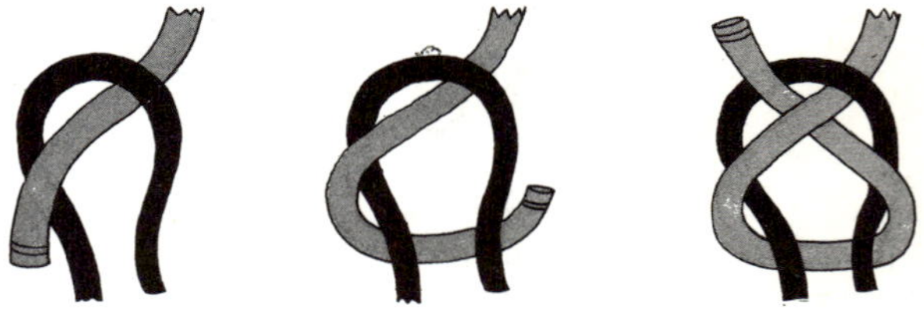

A sheet bend is used whenever you need a knot on a rope that will be under strain.

Round turn and two half-hitches

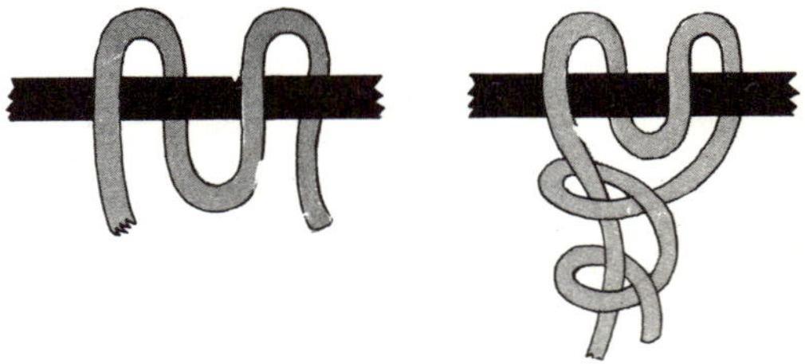

This knot is a useful hitch and it is usually used for tying a rope to a pole. For instance: a washing line or making a boat fast to the bank.

The best way of learning the knots is to keep practising.

See if you can become proficient enough to tie them behind your back!

Bronze Knots

Don't forget you also still have to be able to tie a reef knot and hank a short rope. After all it's no good learning how to tie a knot and then forgetting it, is it?

Scout Link

You will need to know knots for your **Scout Standard.**
Think how many times you will use knots in the Troop: for building bridges and the many other things that the Troop do.

12th Port

The Promise

Show that you have tried to live up to the Promise since you gained your Bronze Arrow.

How long is it since you were invested? One year, two years? What a lot has happened in that time. You have got your Bronze Arrow and you have nearly finished your Silver Arrow. You are a year or so older and perhaps you are a Second or even a Sixer. You have joined in Pack outings and activities.

But one thing hasn't changed. The Cub Scout Law and Promise. It is still exactly the same.

The Law

A Cub Scout always does his best,
thinks of others before himself
and does a good turn every day.

The Promise

I promise that I will do my best
To do my duty to God and to the Queen,
To help other people
and to keep the Cub Scout Law.

It is still a hard Promise to always keep, but as a Cub Scout you made that Promise so you are trying your best and will keep trying your best however hard it is.

Of course you are older now and you know more, so perhaps that makes it a bit easier. How will you show Akela that you have tried very hard to keep your Promise?

Here are some things to ask yourself that might help you to see how well you have kept your Promise.

Have I always helped the younger and weaker boys?

Have I always played the game to the rules and never cheated?

Have I always remembered to say 'thank you' to God for every good thing?

Do I always try to do my best at home, at school and at Pack Meetings?
Do I ever throw litter on the ground?

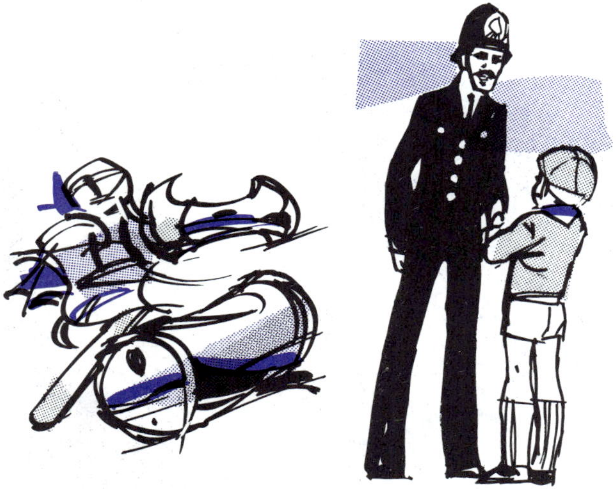

Am I always pleasant to see or am I so busy thinking of myself that I never have time to be pleasant?
How helpful have I been to Mum, Dad, my Brothers and Sisters, Akela and the Pack?
Have I broken many promises?
Have I kept all the laws of the country?

How did you get on? Can you see how you have kept your Promise since your Bronze Arrow? As one of the older Cubs others will be looking to see if you are keeping it.

Here's a card for you to fill in to help you to remember your Promise. Tick off the things as you do them.

Say a prayer for every good thing God as given you.

Do a good turn for Mum, Dad or one of the other members of the family.

Try and be pleasant to somebody you don't like very much (you might even find that you do like them!).

Do a good turn at school.

Think of a prayer you could use at Pack Meetings.

Go for one week without dropping litter, or spoiling any natural thing.

Try and save some pocket money and use it to give to a charity that interests you.

See if you can do a good turn for someone worse off than you are.

Say a special prayer for all boys, who are Cub age in the poorer countries, for peace in the world and for an end to hunger.

Completed

Scout Link to Promise

The Promise in the Troop is the same as your Cub Scout Promise. You will go on right into the Troop trying your best to keep up to the Promise.

When you have completed this you have finished your **Silver Arrow.** Congratulations!

Did you enjoy your **Silver Arrow** voyage? Well you are now going on to even more exciting things in your **Gold Arrow.** You will enjoy that just as much.

Congratulations — Silver Arrow Cub Scout, best of luck with your **Gold Arrow**

This is to certify that I passed my

Silver Arrow

on . . . .

It was presented to me on . . . .

Akela's Signature . . . .